Canada's Road to Independence

Weigl Educational Publishers Limited

Published by Weigl Educational Publishers Limited
6325 – 10 Street SE
Calgary, Alberta, Canada
T2H 2Z9

Web site: www.weigl.com

All of the Internet URLs given in the book were valid at the time of publication.
However, due to the dynamic nature of the Internet, some addresses may have
changed, or sites may have ceased to exist since publication. While the author and
publisher regret any inconvenience this may cause readers, no responsibility for any
such changes can be accepted by either the author or the publisher.

Library and Archives Canada Cataloguing in Publication
    Canada's road to independence / Don Wells, editor.
(Canadian government)
Includes index.
ISBN 1-55388-069-2 (bound) ISBN 1-55388-124-9 (pbk)
    1. Canada--History--Textbooks. I. Wells, Don, 1953- II. Series: Canadian
government (Calgary, Alta.)
FC170.C346 2004   971   C2004-903628-9

Printed in the United States of America
1 2 3 4 5 6 7 8 9 0   09 08 07 06 05 04

We acknowledge the
financial support of the
Government of Canada
through the Book
Publishing Industry
Development Program
(BPIDP) for our
publishing activities.

Editor
Don Wells

Copy Editor
Heather C. Hudak

Photo Researcher
Ellen Byran

Designer
Warren Clark

Layout
Terry Paulhus

On the Cover
Prime Minister Pierre
Trudeau and Queen
Elizabeth II signed
Canada's constitutional
proclamation in 1982.

Contents

Canadian Sovereignty

Canada is a constitutional monarch, which means the Queen of Canada reigns, but does not rule.

■ Elizabeth II became queen in 1953. She succeeded her father King George VI.

Within the framework of democracy, Canada has evolved from a country ruled by a distant **monarch** into a sovereign, or independent, land. A sovereign nation has the legal power to control its territory, including land, water, and air space. It also has the legal right to make decisions on behalf of its citizens.

Canada is a constitutional monarchy, which means the Queen of Canada reigns, but does not rule. Elections are called, and laws are passed in the monarch's name. All government legislators, public servants, and members of the military and police forces swear allegiance to the Queen rather than Canada's flag or Constitution.

Early Canada was made up of a group of British **colonies**—Nova Scotia, New Brunswick, Prince Edward Island, and the United Province of Canada. Today, the United Province of Canada is known as Ontario and Québec. Together, these colonies were known as the British North American colonies. These early Canadian settlements were weak and nearly defenceless. They invested most of their energy into making their settlements successful and surviving the hardships of North America. The British North American colonies relied on Great Britain for protection, allowing British authorities to negotiate treaties and agreements on their behalf.

Unfortunately, many of Great Britain's negotiations did not reflect a strong knowledge of or concern for the colonies'—which are now known as Canada—needs and interests. Most of the time, international negotiations reflected Great Britain's own priorities. Without the authority to conduct its own negotiations, Canada often found itself on the losing side of disputes. A conflict over borders on San Juan Island shows how disputes were not always resolved in Canada's favour or best interest.

Early Canada was often involved in boundary

disputes with the United States. Some borders had been drawn through little-known regions, resulting in disputable boundary lines. In 1846, Great Britain signed a treaty with America extending the border between Canada and the United States west of the Rocky Mountains. The boundary line followed the 49th parallel to the middle of the straits separating Vancouver Island from the mainland. In 1857, a conflict arose regarding the many islands in these straits. Both the Territory of Washington and Vancouver Island claimed the island of San Juan and placed customs officials on it.

One day an American settler living on San Juan killed a pig that had wandered onto his property. The animal belonged to the Hudson's Bay Company. Expecting the Canadian company to retaliate against the U.S. for the man's actions, the United States sent a small force of troops to occupy the island. In response, the governor of Vancouver Island called on the British navy to expel the American troops. Quick negotiations resulted in compromise. Both Canada and the U.S. were allowed to station 100 men on the island.

In 1872, the San Juan dispute was settled, and the island was awarded to the Americans. Canadians were angered by the loss of San Juan Island, and many began to feel the first stirrings of the need for **sovereignty**.

The San Juan Boundary Dispute 1871–72

British claim
British compromise
United States' claim
(Boundary as awarded 1872)

Mouth of Fraser R.

Point Roberts

Boundary Bay

Saturna I.

Sidney

Orcas I.

Haro Strait

Fidalgo I.

Victoria

Rosario Strait

San Juan I.

N

0   65 km

FURTHER UNDERSTANDING

Democracy

Democracy is a form of government that is ruled by the people. Democracy can be either direct or representative. Ancient Athens was a direct democracy, where the people voted on laws and other issues. Today, most democratic societies elect representatives to form a government that acts on behalf of the people. Most democratic societies value freedom and equality for their citizens. Three key freedoms of democracy are freedom of speech, freedom of the press, and freedom of religion.

Steps to Confederation

Most Loyalists came to what is now Canada in 1783 and 1784.

While the United States gained independence from Great Britain through a swift and angry revolution, the Canadian movement toward sovereignty took more than 100 years.

Part of this lengthy process was the result of Canada's inheritance of British Loyalists during the American Revolution. In the aftermath of the revolution, a large number of Loyalists fled from the United States into Canada, resulting in a Canadian population that was relatively loyal to Great Britain and its empire. The Loyalists were not eager to push quickly for separation from Great Britain because they had just defended the Empire at great cost during the American Revolution (1775–1783).

Another reason for the slow pace of Canadian sovereignty was the reluctance by each British North American colony to find common interests with their neighbours. Many of the colonial leaders had a difficult time convincing their citizens of the benefits of a united country. However, without unity, the British colonies lacked the power to be completely independent of Great Britain's protection and guidance.

While specific concerns with unity varied, most colonies feared a loss of **autonomy**. All the colonies had a great deal of independence in their internal affairs at the time of Confederation. The United Province of Canada, consisting of the mostly English-speaking Canada West and the mostly French-speaking Canada East, was not united in its views about a potential federation. Canada West was generally supportive. Canada East feared a system of representative democracy because their French-speaking population was smaller than the combined population

of the English-speaking colonies. New Brunswick had little contact with the rest of Canada. New Brunswick had established strong trade links with the United States; only 3 percent of its trade was with the rest of Canada. Like New Brunswick, Nova Scotia and Prince Edward Island (PEI) worried that their interests would be lost in a union because of their small populations.

In September, 1864, delegates from Nova Scotia, New Brunswick, and PEI planned to meet in Charlottetown to discuss the idea of a Maritime union. Only Charles Tupper, premier of Nova Scotia, was enthusiastic about the prospect of a union. Nova Scotia was the most populated Maritime colony at this time. Tupper believed he would be an important leader once the colonies united.

When the other Canadian colonies heard about the meeting, they requested an invitation to present their idea to unite all the British North American colonies. Once the Maritime colonies heard the proposal, they discarded their plans for a Maritime union. The Charlottetown meeting was a success, and the delegates agreed to meet again to discuss specifics of the plan.

Delegates from each of the colonies met a month later in Québec City to draw up a plan for the new country. During the Québec Conference, each colony lobbied for its own interests. Newfoundland sent a representative to the Québec meeting, although they had not been present at Charlottetown.

In 1864, the delegates took the Québec Resolutions back to their colonies. The proposal was hotly debated in each colony. In 1865, the United Province of Canada passed the proposal with a wide majority, although there were dissenting votes from French-speaking Canada East. Nova Scotia and New Brunswick only accepted the plan after significant political pressure by Great Britain. Following the provincial election after Confederation, Nova Scotians defeated Charles Tupper and even tried to repeal their acceptance into Confederation. Both PEI and Newfoundland turned down Confederation.

PROFILE

Sir John Alexander Macdonald

Sir John A. Macdonald, Canada's first prime minister, was born in Glasgow, Scotland, in January, 1815. When Macdonald was 5 years old, his parents immigrated to what is now Kingston, Ontario. By the time he was 19, he had opened his own law office in Kingston. In 1844, at the age of 29, Macdonald was elected to the Legislative Assembly of the Province of Canada.

From 1864 until his death, Macdonald devoted much of his time to the creation of a new constitution, a document that would be passed into law as the British North America Act (BNA Act). On July 1, 1867, Macdonald was named prime minister of the newly-formed **Dominion** of Canada. He oversaw a period of "nation-building."

In 1874, Macdonald was forced to resign over a scandal regarding campaign financing, but he returned to power in 1878. During this term, the Transcontinental Railroad was completed, an action which guaranteed the inclusion of British Columbia into the Dominion of Canada. This made the motto of the Dominion of Canada—*A mari usque ad mari* (from sea to sea)—a reality.

Sir John A. Macdonald died at age 76 of heart failure. He is buried in Kingston, Ontario.

British North America Act

Following the Québec Conference in 1864, the Québec Resolutions were taken to London where the Westminster Conference accepted them as the basic plan for the union. In March 1867, the British Parliament passed the plan, calling it the British North America Act (BNA Act). Confederation officially took place on July 1, 1867.

The British North America Act of 1867 changed Canada's colonial status. This document united the colonies and gave them internal self-rule. Although the colonies proposed to call themselves the Kingdom of Canada, Great Britain suggested that the name Dominion of Canada would antagonize the Americans less. Following their independence from Great Britain, the Americans were still sensitive about the British Empire's presence in North America.

The British North America Act—now called the Constitution Act 1867—had the following provisions:
- The lieutenant-governors of the provinces will be appointed and

FURTHER UNDERSTANDING

Governor General of Canada

Legally, the governor general represents the Queen, who is the head of state. He or she calls the sitting of Parliament, must approve all laws passed by Parliament, and is commander-in-chief of the Canadian Armed Forces. However, the real power rests with the prime minister, the parliament, and the provincial governments. The governor general's job is ceremonial. He or she attends banquets and state functions and gives awards such as the Order of Canada. The governor general is named by the Queen, but the prime minister chooses who will be named to this position. The position alternates between English and French Canadians. This is a tradition that is an unwritten part of Canada's Constitution.

Canada's Coat of Arms replaced the Royal Arms of the United Kingdom in 1921.

DOCUMENT

An Act for the Union of Canada, Nova Scotia, and New Brunswick, and the Government thereof; and for the purposes connected therewith. (29th March, 1867)

Whereas the Provinces of Canada, Nova Scotia, and New Brunswick have expressed their desire to be... united into One Dominion under the **Crown** of the United Kingdom of Great Britain and Ireland, with a Constitution similar... to that of the United Kingdom:

And whereas such a Union would conduce to the Welfare of the Provinces and promote the Interests of the British Empire:

And whereas it is expedient that Provision be made for the eventual admission into the Union of other Parts of British North America: Be it therefore enacted and declared by the Queens' most Excellent Majesty, by and with the advice and Consent of the Lords Spiritual and Temporal, and Commons, in this present Parliament assembled, and by the Authority of the sames, as follows:
1. This Act may be cited as the British North America Act 1867.

paid by the federal government and can, on federal instruction, send any provincial bill to the governor general to reject or accept.

- The governor general can reject any provincial law within 1 year of receiving a copy of the law.
- The federal government has unlimited taxing powers. The provinces are limited to direct taxes within the province.
- Parliament can assume responsibility for any project, even though it is located in only one province, if it is considered important to Canada or two or more provinces.

Although the 1867 Constitution created a strong central government, Québec's unique character was recognized, and the use of French and the province's civil law was given official status.

Canada's leaders formed a confederation in order to cope with the major constitutional and economic problems of the late nineteenth century. This confederation combined parliamentary government and **federalism** in a completely new way. The Canadian model influenced Australia and several other federations.

The BNA Act created a Canadian Constitution based on the British parliamentary system as well as British laws. The Act also made provision for the entry of new provinces into Confederation.

Great Britain retained control over Canadian defence and foreign affairs, and Canada was still subject to the laws Great Britain exercised over its empire. Great Britain controlled Canada through the governor general.

HISTORY

Silent Voices

The Aboriginal and Inuit Peoples have lived in North America for thousands of years, but by the time of Confederation, the European settlers had moved many Aboriginal Peoples onto small areas of land called reserves. The government tried to make Aboriginal Peoples live like Europeans. Although today it is not right for one group to change another group's way of life, in the 1860s, people did not consider this to be wrong. In addition to trying to assimilate Aboriginal Peoples, Canadian leaders did not include them in discussions about Confederation. As a result, Aboriginal Peoples had no say over the future of the land they had lived on for thousands of years.

Women were also excluded from discussions about Confederation. In 1867, women were not allowed to be politicians or vote in federal elections. Canadian women did not receive the right to vote in federal elections until 1918. Women gained the right to be elected to the House of Commons in 1919.

■ *Some Aboriginal Peoples, such as this group of Cree, had to work as labourers to earn money to buy food.*

Steps to Sovereignty 1867–1945

To some, Canada's development as an independent nation may appear unspectacular.

■ *About 100,000 people headed north in the fall and winter of 1897 in search of gold. Money to fund their explorations boosted Canada's struggling economy.*

Canadian sovereignty has been defined by incidents and resolutions rather than by revolutions. To some, Canada's development as an independent nation may appear unspectacular. There were no large-scale wars of independence or civil unrest. Slow but steady growth took place from 1867 to 1945 as Canada became an increasingly independent country in the years leading up to and including World War I and World War II.

In 1871, Canada made progress toward greater independence when all British troops were withdrawn from the country. Sir John A. Macdonald's presence at the negotiating table during the Treaty of Washington was another small acknowledgment of Canada's emerging independence. Despite these acknowledgments, the years leading to

World War I were filled with events that tested the ability of Canada and Great Britain to defend Canadian territory from American interests.

Canada's resource-based economy meant the financial well-being of the country depended on trade. In 1880, Canada appointed its first high commissioner to London. Canada's commissioner, however, was not allowed to sign trade treaties. Still, Canada continued to send trade commissioners to Europe and, in doing so, maintained a presence and voice in negotiations.

Canada's border with the United States, which once led to the brink of war over San Juan Island, was again the focus of dispute over the Alaska boundary. Before the United States purchased Alaska from Russia, the

boundary between Alaska and Canada was established by a Russian-British agreement. Unfortunately, the Russian-British agreement was unclear about exactly where the boundary was located.

British Columbia is separated from the Pacific Ocean by a narrow strip of land known as the Alaskan Panhandle. Until the Klondike Gold Rush in the late 1890s, few people were interested in this region. However, much of the Klondike gold was located in the Canadian Yukon, and the easiest route to this area was through the Panhandle.

During the gold rush, a temporary agreement between Canada and the United States accepted the city of Skagway, Alaska, as American. Miners crossed American territory until they reached a Royal Canadian Mounted Police outpost, which was the boundary of Canadian territory. This agreement proved unsatisfactory to Canada and the United States.

Great Britain and the United States agreed to ask three impartial judges from each country to provide a solution. When the vote was taken on October 17, 1903, Lord Alverstone, a British judge acting for Canada, sided with the three Americans, and the boundary favoured by the Americans was upheld.

Canada became more independent during the Boer War. In 1899, Great Britain and the Boer republics in South Africa went to war. The Boers, descendants of Dutch explorers, sought independence from British rule, while the British wished to retain control over the diamond- and gold-rich territory. Great Britain required assistance and asked Canada and the other Dominions to help. Canada itself was not in danger, and many Canadians believed Canada should not become involved in Great Britain's affairs.

Faced with this resistance, Prime Minister Wilfrid Laurier, Canada's first Francophone prime minister, decided to send a volunteer army to the war rather than an official army. Approximately 8,000 troops volunteered and were equipped by the Canadian government.

Canadian autonomy was asserted during the war. Canadian troops served in British regiments as separate Canadians units. Canadian soldiers fought well and gained respect for both themselves and their country.

In January 1900, Donald Smith, or Lord Strathcona, equipped a mounted regiment to fight in the Boer War at his own expense.

FURTHER UNDERSTANDING
The Naval Bill 1910

In 1910, the Naval Bill was passed, creating a small Canadian navy of two training cruisers. This navy, although meant to bolster Great Britain's defensive force in the face of German munitions manufacturing, was fairly insignificant as a potential war tool. Its real significance was that it remained in control of Canadian rather than British policymakers. Just as in the Boer War, however, French and English interests viewed Canada's fledgling navy differently. English supporters called the small naval service a "tin-pot navy," and argued that Great Britain needed much greater help. For French Canadians, the new navy was a move toward **conscription** of their young men into British imperial wars.

Canada in World War I

On July 5, 1915, the Canadian government formed the Number 2 Construction Battalion. All the soldiers in this unit were Canadians of African descent.

At the beginning of 1914, Canada had many reasons to be optimistic. The Canadian economy was beginning to flourish. Canadians were hopeful about their future. The theme of the Toronto National Exhibition that year was "Peace."

In August 1914, World War I, the "War to End All Wars," began. Canada did not declare war in this conflict. Legally, Canada could not declare war without Great Britain's permission. When Great Britain declared war against Germany, Canada, as a Dominion in the British Empire, was bound by that decision and forced to declare war.

Sir Wilfrid Laurier said it was natural for Canada to respond to the Empire's need with firm resolve. At the beginning of the war, Prime Minister Robert Borden's government passed the War Measures Act. The Act gives the government special powers in times of national crisis. The Act allows the government to suspend citizens' legal rights, including freedom of assembly and freedom of expression.

During the war, the government used the Act to control individuals thought to present a threat to Canadian security. These people were stripped of their rights and property. More than 8,000 Ukrainian Canadians were uprooted from their farms and businesses in western Canada and sent to work camps in other parts of the country. Many Germans and Austrians were fired from their jobs. In the rush to separate itself from anything related to Germany, the city of Berlin, Ontario, changed its name to Kitchener.

At the start of the war, Canada had 3,000 soldiers and a small navy. Charged with raising an army, Sir Sam Hughes,

Minister of the Militia, took charge of recruitment. By the beginning of October, 1914, 30,000 Canadian volunteers were assembled. These troops were both poorly equipped and inadequately trained. Recruitment continued throughout 1914 and 1915. Many young Canadians joined the army out of patriotism, a pride in and love of their country.

By the end of the war, there were 620,000 Canadians in the army, 425,000 of whom went overseas. In a country with a population of only eight million, Canada's wartime contribution was extremely significant.

Canadians arriving in England for dispatch to the front were placed under the control of the British army. Still, Canadian soldiers distinguished themselves and their country in the trenches of Europe.

HISTORY

Canadian Heroes in World War I

Billy Bishop

Baron von Richtoffen, the Red Baron, leads the list of World War I "air aces" with 80 confirmed kills. He is followed by Rene Fonck of France, who had 75 air victories. The third greatest air ace of World War I was Canadian William (Billy) Bishop, who had 72 confirmed victories. Bishop, who was the British Empire's top fighter pilot, had a tendency to crash his plane upon landing, but by the end of the war, he was a celebrated fighter ace. Of the top six fighter pilots flying for Great Britain during the war,

■ *Billy Bishop received the Victoria Cross for bravery in battle.*

four were Canadian. In addition to Bishop were Raymond Collishaw (60 victories), Donald Maclaren (54 victories), and William Barker (50 victories). Unlike many other pilots, Bishop survived the war. He lived until 1956.

Arthur Currie

Arthur Currie was commander of the Canadian First Division and, later, the entire Canadian contingent in France. Before the war, he had worked as a businessperson, an insurance salesperson, and a school teacher. When the war began, he enlisted in the militia and worked his way through the ranks to become a lieutenant colonel of the artillery. Although he was not a professional soldier, he had a deep interest in his troops' health and safety and a strong belief in preparation and training. His concern not only saved many Canadian lives, but it also helped the Canadian forces achieve many victories. His training and attention to detail were two of the main reasons for Canada's success at Vimy Ridge—a heavily defended area in northern France that protected German factories—in April 1917. He was an intelligent commander who was always willing to learn from the experiences of his troops and the troops of other nations. He remains one of Canada's greatest military commanders.

Francis Pegahmagabow

Francis Pegahmagabow was the son of the Chief of the Parry Island Band of the Ojibwa Nation. He enlisted in the Canadian army at the beginning of the war and served until it ended. Even though he was shot in the leg at Ypres, he returned to fight. His actions in battle earned him the Military Medal with two bars—meaning he earned the same medal three times. Many Canadian Aboriginal Peoples served with distinction in the Canadian army. Pegahmagabow became Chief of the Parry Island Band of the Ojibwa Nation. He lived until 1952.

Outcome of World War I

In 1917, at the Battle of Vimy Ridge, Canadian soldiers formed a separate fighting unit within the British army. Using tunnels, the Canadians captured this strategically important post. The Canadian feat at Vimy Ridge was noteworthy because the ridge had resisted three previous attacks. After Vimy, Canadian troops were placed under the command of Canadian Arthur Currie. This was a vote of confidence for Canada's abilities and contributions on the battleground.

Canadian bravery came at a high price. More than 10,000 Canadian soldiers were wounded, and more than 3,000 died at Vimy Ridge.

By this time, the war was into its third year, and casualty rates soared. By January 1916, Prime Minister Borden had increased Canadian commitment to the war to 500,000 troops. Most of these soldiers were recent British **immigrants**.

The war did not receive much support in French Canada. French Canadians felt only distantly connected to France and Europe. They did not feel any connection to Great Britain and its causes.

This French-Canadian resistance to the war increased French-English tensions in Canada. Many English Canadians pushed for **conscription,** or involuntary recruitment of soldiers.

The Canadian corps fought as a unit under Canadian command for the first time at Vimy Ridge.

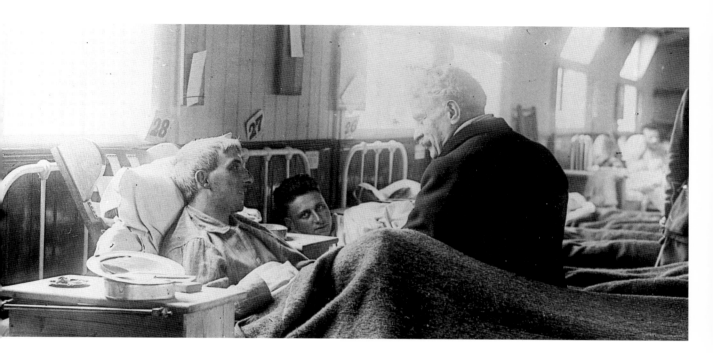

The government passed the War Times Election Act, which gave the vote to widows, wives, mothers, daughters, and sisters of Canadian soldiers overseas. The vote was also given to all men and women serving in the forces. Clearly, such additions to the electorate would likely support a move to conscription.

To preserve Canadian honour, and to prevent wounded soldiers from being sent back to fight, Prime Minister Borden introduced conscription in August 1917. Québec reacted with riots. The Conscription Crisis almost tore the country apart. French and English Canadians remembered this crisis with resentment.

As casualties from the war increased, and the war lasted longer than predicted, Canada and the other British Dominions demanded more input into war planning. At the Imperial War Conference in 1917, Great Britain formed the Imperial War Cabinet. This cabinet consisted of Great Britain's prime minister and the prime minister of each self-governing Dominion. At the first conference, the cabinet announced that the Dominions were equal partners with Great Britain. At this point, Great Britain began dealing directly with Canada's External Affairs Department.

Aside from facilitating political sovereignty from Great Britain, the events of World War I allowed Canada to grow stronger and more independent. Agriculture boomed as Canadian farms grew wheat to feed the British armies. Factories produced munitions and machinery, women worked in factories to satisfy a labour shortage, and rations for food and other materials important to the war effort became commonplace methods for supporting the war.

Another significant measure was the Income Tax Act of 1917. This tax was passed to help pay Canada's war costs, and it was intended to be a temporary solution.

In 1917, Sir Robert Borden visited the western front and spoke with wounded soldiers.

Canada's Growing Independence

At the end of World War I, a conference to draw up peace treaties was held at Versailles, France. Canada had made a greater contribution to the war than some fully independent nations, and it demanded a seat at the negotiations. Some nations objected to Canada's participation. They saw Canada as a British puppet which would only reinforce Great Britain's position at the conference. Despite these objections, the Dominions were granted separate representation. Canada's presence at Versailles was an indication of Canada's growing international independence.

This growth was consolidated in 1919, when Canada was admitted to the League of Nations. By signing the Treaty of Versailles, Canada automatically received League membership. The League of Nations was a multinational organization whose goal was to prevent war through collective security.

Despite its heroic war participation, Canada was basically isolationist in its foreign policy during the 1920s. This meant that Canada preferred a policy of caring for its own affairs and leaving other nations to do the same. Canada's location in the world placed it far from the dangers of Europe. Canada did not, therefore, share Europe's concern for collective security.

Events in 1922 demonstrated Canada's ability to act independently of British control. Great Britain and Turkey were on the verge of war over Chanak, an area in the Dardanelles. Great Britain, as it had in the past, requested Canada to prepare troops. However, because

Canada had become more independent, many believed Great Britain should no longer have the right to mobilize Canadian soldiers. Canadian Prime Minister William Lyon Mackenzie King and his government wanted it to be clear to Great Britain that Canadian participation in British conflicts would be on a volunteer basis only. Compounding matters, Winston Churchill, Great Britain's Colonial Secretary, issued a press release appealing directly to the Canadian public to obtain support for Canadian involvement in the war. Annoyed that his government was bypassed, King stated he would first need to consult with Parliament before troops could be sent.

The Chanak affair was important to Canadian sovereignty for several reasons. The disagreement showed how Great Britain's and Canada's interests were growing apart. It also showed flaws in the methods used by Great Britain to keep its Empire together. Great Britain favoured central control over imperial policy. It consulted with the Dominions when necessary. The Canadian hesitation to enter a conflict with Turkey at Great Britain's request demonstrated that self-interest was now the rule when the Dominions made decisions about their future.

Under King, the Canadian government continued to make independent decisions. In 1923, King sent a Canadian representative to Washington to sign the Halibut Treaty with the United States. The treaty agreed to a closed fishing season in the north Pacific. Although Canada had been negotiating its own commercial treaties for years, British officials were still summoned to sign final agreements. By refusing Great Britain's offer to sign for Canada, a precedent was set which allowed the colonies of the Empire more independence relations.

■ Winston Churchill served as the British Colonial Secretary from 1921 to 1922.

FURTHER UNDERSTANDING

League of Nations

The idea for the League of Nations originated with British Foreign Secretary Edward Grey, and it was supported by U.S. President Woodrow Wilson and his advisor Colonel Edward House. These leaders believed the League could help the world avoid the bloodshed that occurred during World War I. Wilson thought the League should be included in the Treaty of Versailles, and the League of Nations was established on January 25, 1919, by part I of the Treaty of Versailles. The League held its first meeting on January 10, 1920, and its first act was to verify the Treaty of Versailles, which officially ended World War I. The first general assembly of the League was held in Geneva on November 15, 1920. The League successfully managed minor conflicts throughout the 1920s. However, it was unable to prevent World War II. The League formally dissolved itself on April 18, 1946, in order to make way for the United Nations.

Canada's Self-interest

In 1921, Canada nominated Julian H. G. Byng for governor general. It was the first time Canada was consulted about the choice of a governor general.

In 1926, Canada's first minister was appointed to the United States. From this point, a Canadian representative spoke on behalf of Canada's interests in Washington, D.C., the U.S. capital.

A second important event in 1926 was the King-Byng Crisis. Prime Minister Mackenzie King's minority government faced defeat in the House of Commons over a customs scandal. King approached Governor General Sir Julian Hedworth George Byng and asked for the dissolution of Parliament. Byng refused King's request because King had only been in power for 9 months. When King resigned, the leader of the Conservative Party, Arthur Meighen, was asked to form the government. In a few days, Meighen faced the same situation King had when he was defeated in the House of Commons. However, when Meighen asked Byng to call an election, he complied.

During the following election, King led his party back to victory by making an issue of Byng's interference. King proclaimed his victory in the election as a victory for Canadian autonomy.

Soon after the King-Byng Crisis, Canada worked for constitutional recognition of its increasing autonomy. At the 1926 Imperial Conference, Canada joined forces with other Dominions to produce the Balfour

Report. As a result of the Balfour Report, the governor general became a representative of the Crown, not an active agent of the British government. The Balfour Report made the role of the governor general more ceremonial and symbolic than politically significant.

Legal independence for Canada occurred in 1931 with the Statute of Westminster. This British document recognized the control of the Dominions over all their affairs. The Statute formalized the idea of a Commonwealth of Nations rather than a British Empire.

The Statute did not, however, recognize sovereignty for the Dominions. The British Parliament still had the power to change the BNA Act or Statute of Westminster. By this time, however, it was highly unlikely that the British Parliament would ever do so without the request of a Dominion.

After the Statute of Westminster was signed, Canada took more action to establish legal autonomy. In 1947, Canada dropped the "Dominion of" from its name. In 1949, the Supreme Court of Canada became the final court of appeal for all criminal and civil cases. Formerly, it was possible to appeal legal cases to the Judicial Committee of the Privy Council in London.

By 1932, the effects of a worldwide Depression were being felt all over the world. When the Commonwealth nations met at the Ottawa Conference on Trade, an important topic of debate was whether the Commonwealth countries should have preferential trade agreements with each other.

After Canada negotiated a preferential treaty with Great Britain, many other Dominions followed suit. This was an important step

toward sovereignty. Each nation in the Commonwealth now put their self-interest ahead of allegiance to Great Britain.

PROFILE

William Lyon Mackenzie King

Canada's tenth Prime Minister, William Lyon Mackenzie King, was born on December 17, 1874, in Kitchener, Ontario. He was first elected to Parliament in 1908, and in 1921 became prime minister. He served three terms as prime minister, for a total of nearly 22 years, making him Canada's longest serving prime minister.

In his first term, he raised questions about the role of the governor general and helped define Canadian sovereignty and Great Britain's role in that sovereignty.

His third term as prime minister, from 1935 to 1948, challenged Great Britain's role even further. King took deliberate steps to distance Canada from Great Britain, which still treated Canada as a colony in many ways. At the beginning of World War II, King called Parliament to an emergency session to decide whether Canada should declare war on Germany. Previously, all former British colonies had automatically been at war once Great Britain declared its involvement.

■ *William Lyon Mackenzie King was defeated and lost power in 1926 and 1930.*

King's legacy to Canada includes such measures as unemployment insurance, family allowances, and the initial proposal for federally sponsored health care.

In 1950, at age 75, King died of pneumonia just 2 years after his retirement from politics.

Canada and the Start of World War II

At the beginning of World War II, Canada sent only a few soldiers, food, and manufactured goods to the war effort.

■ After France fell in 1940, the Canadian armed forces were quickly expanded. Conscription was introduced in 1940 for home defence, and the government greatly increased its spending.

The economic concerns of the 1930s made it difficult for Canada to react to the "decade of aggression." When Japan invaded Manchuria in 1931, Canada expressed only concern and a willingness to discuss the problem. Similarly, when Italy invaded Ethiopia in 1935, the Canadian government agreed only to support any resolution determined by the League of Nations.

Great Britain and France followed a policy of appeasement in the 1930s. Through appeasement, the countries believed that granting legitimate demands would prevent war. At the Imperial Conference of 1937, Canada supported the British appeasement policy. When this policy allowed Germany's Adolf Hitler to take control of the Sudetenland in 1938, Canada did not interfere. Mackenzie King even visited Hitler after the Imperial Conference and came back reassured that the world had nothing to fear.

However, Hitler took control of Czechoslovakia in 1939, after much of that country had been handed over to European countries during the Munich Crisis of 1938. Soon after, on September 1, 1939, Hitler invaded Poland.

Following the Polish invasion, Great Britain declared war on Germany. Unlike the British declaration which signalled Canadian involvement in World War I, Canada was not automatically at war with Great Britain's declaration. The Statute of Westminster had made Canada and the other Dominions independent of the British government. As a result, it was not until 1 week later that Canada declared war on Germany. With the announcement, Prime Minister Mackenzie King reassured the country that conscription would not be used.

Initially, Canada sent only a few soldiers, food, and manufactured goods to the war effort. However, after the fall of France in 1940, it appeared that Germany would soon threaten Great Britain. More and more Canadian troops were called upon to fight in the war. Volunteers raced to enlist. After the first month, Canada had an army of 55,000 people.

Recruiting and coordinating wartime production were immediate Canadian priorities. As Germany increased its air attacks on Great Britain, Canadian munition supplies became essential to the war effort. As they did in World War I, Canadian factories began to increase production, and unemployment disappeared. Sugar, meat, and gasoline rationing were introduced. An enormous number of women entered the labour force to make up for labour shortages. Women entered virtually every area of the manufacturing and service industries to keep the home front functioning efficiently.

HISTORY

Canada's Warrior Women

Jerry Mumford

Jerry Mumford was from a service corps in Halifax. She was sent to Great Britain during 1940. Mumford helped put out fires and assisted people with injuries while bombs fell on London. She was one of the few women selected to travel to Italy with the Canadian army in 1944. Mumford worked, occasionally without sleep, to bring wounded troops to safety.

■ *The Canadian Women's Army Corps was established on August 13, 1941.*

Maude Elizabeth Steen

Maude Elizabeth Steen became a radio operator after training in Canada. Female radio operators were only allowed to travel to the war effort on ships from Norway. She made her way onto a Norwegian ship, the S.S. Viggo Hansteen. Ten weeks after she signed on board the ship, it was torpedoed by a German submarine. Steen lost her life helping deliver troops for the war effort.

Canada in World War II

By 1941, more than 250,000 men and some 2,000 women had joined the Canadian army.

■ *Atomic bombs were dropped on Japan in World War II. Since then, nuclear weapons have not been used in war.*

In 1940, the Canadian and American governments signed the Ogdensburg Agreement, which created a Permanent Joint Board of Defence for the entire North American continent. This agreement was significant because it showed a shift in Canada's traditional alliance with Great Britain to acknowledge a common interest base with its American neighbours. As part of the agreement, the United States pledged to defend Canada from invaders.

In a second agreement, the 1941 Hyde Park Agreement, the United States agreed to continue sending war supplies to Canada. This agreement helped ease Canada's cash flow problems caused by the war.

By 1941, more than 250,000 men and some 2,000 women had joined the army. The December 1941 Japanese attack on the U.S. naval base at Pearl Harbor in Hawai'i and the fall of Hong Kong brought the war close to home. The possibility of an attack on North America now seemed possible. Many people on the home front panicked, encouraging Canada to increase its war effort. Under the terms of the War Measures Act, thousands of Japanese

PROFILE

Joy Kogawa

Japanese-Canadian writer Joy Kogawa was born in 1935 in Vancouver, British Columbia. Her novel, *Obasan*, brought her international acclaim. *Obasan* tells the story of the evacuation, internment, and dispersal of Japanese Canadians in Canada during World War II. Kogawa's family was uprooted in 1942 when the entire west coast region relocated any person of Japanese origin to remote areas of western Canada. The Kogawa family was relocated to Slocan, in the interior of British Columbia.

At the end of World War II, the dislocated Japanese Canadians were not allowed to return to their homes. They were told either to settle in the Rocky Mountains in British Columbia or return to Japan.

 *Joy Kogawa tells a simple story about her internment camp experience in her children's book, Naomi's Road.*

The Kogawa family moved to Coaldale, Alberta, where they lived in a one-room hut without electricity or water. At 20, Joy studied music at the Royal Conservatory of Music in Toronto and began writing in her late twenties. *Obasan* was published in 1981, and it has become an important testimony to the hardships suffered by Japanese Canadians during World War II.

FURTHER UNDERSTANDING

Manhattan Project

In 1942, the United States government started the Manhattan Project. This project was formed to develop an atomic bomb. There were fears that Germany was close to producing nuclear weapons. The first nuclear chain reaction occurred at the University of Chicago in 1942. The first test atomic bomb was detonated on July 16, 1945 at Alamogordo, New Mexico. President Harry S. Truman ordered the first atomic bomb dropped on Hiroshima, Japan, on August 6, 1945. A second atomic bomb was dropped on Nagasaki, Japan, 3 days later. Japan surrendered on August 14, 1945. It took 175,000 people to develop and build the first atomic bombs. The Manhattan Project cost $2 billion.

Canadians were sent to internment camps in the interior of British Columbia or southern Alberta. Some feared Japanese Canadians would act as spies for a forthcoming Japanese invasion of North America.

On April 27, 1942, Prime Minister Mackenzie King announced a referendum that allowed Canadians to vote on the issue of conscription. English Canada voted 79 percent in favour of conscription, and French Canada voted 72 percent against conscription. On June 10, 1942, King's government passed Bill 80, which allowed for conscription. On November 22, 1944, King invoked conscription. This time, conscription did not divide the country as it had in World War I.

On June 6, 1944, the final assault on Hitler's Europe began. Operation Overlord, or D-Day, comprised some 300,000 soldiers, 4,000 ships and 11,000 aircraft. After almost 1 year of fighting, Germany surrendered on May 7, 1945.

The war continued in the Pacific. The Japanese did not know that a team of international scientists had created a new weapon—the atomic bomb. The war against Japan ended on August 6, 1945, when one of these bombs was dropped on the city of Hiroshima. The bomb had a destructive force of 20,000 tonnes of TNT. More than 80,000 people were killed almost instantly. Three days later a second bomb was dropped on the city of Nagasaki, and another 60,000 people were killed. These two bombs ended World War II and ushered in the Atomic Age.

Postwar Canada

When Germany, Japan, and their allies were defeated in 1945, Canada joined the United States, the United Kingdom, the Soviet Union, and China as signatories of the treaties that marked the end of the war. Canada's actions in the postwar world gave birth to the term *middle power*, a country which exercises influence, but which cannot alone determine international affairs. Canada's involvement with other nations after World War II would play an important part in its sovereignty.

World War II caused serious economic and political problems in Europe and Japan. The world powers wanted to avoid an economic depression similar to that of 1929, which, in some ways, may have contributed to World War II. In order to solve the economic and political problems caused by World War II, a conference was held in 1944 at Bretton Woods, New Hampshire. At that conference, the International Monetary Fund (IMF) and the International Bank for Reconstruction and Development (IBRD) were established. The IMF provided short-term loans to countries with currency problems. The IBRD, now commonly known as the World Bank, provided long-term loans for development. Canada supported both agencies.

The Commonwealth created the Colombo Plan in 1950. This plan provided assistance for the economic development of Commonwealth countries. The plan was seen as a **humanitarian** gesture and a means of stopping **communism**. By the

■ *While Europe suffered economically after World War II, Canadian industry boomed. An enormous oil field was discovered in Leduc, Alberta. The discovery created a new industry in the province.*

mid-1950s, Canada was recognized as a leading Commonwealth member.

The economic ruin of Europe and Japan left many markets open to North American goods and services. Canada's manufacturing industry thrived. The discovery of massive oil fields in central Alberta in 1947 brought prosperity to the West and greatly expanded resource development in the area.

In 1945, Canada was the fourth largest western power. Geographically, Canada's location placed it in a position to take advantage of both the Atlantic and Pacific trade areas. Canada was also located on a direct route between Washington, D.C. and Moscow, and as the Cold War developed between the two superpowers, Canada sometimes found itself literally caught in the middle.

The postwar era meant new challenges to Canadian sovereignty. Great Britain was no longer a threat to Canada's plans for independence. Thriving American economic and military power, however, did exert influence and, in some cases, domination over Canadian sovereignty.

IN-DEPTH

Canada's Flag

Before 1965, Canada did not have an official flag. When France ruled Canada, the royal banner of France was flown. This flag showed three fleurs-de-lis, or irises, on a blue background. Québec's provincial flag also has the fleur-de-lis.

When Canada came under British control in 1760, two British flags were flown: Great Britain's Union Flag, or the Union Jack, and the Canadian Red Ensign. The Union Jack is the British flag. The Canadian Red Ensign was the flag of the British merchant marine. It is a red flag with the Union Jack in the upper left corner and a shield on the right side.

These flags did not consider Aboriginal **symbols**. Before and after contact with Europeans, Aboriginal Peoples had symbols for unity and **identity**. There was great **diversity** among Aboriginal Peoples. Some of their symbols included eagle feathers, the sacred pipe, painted shields, and painted teepees. These symbols identified families, clans, and tribes.

In the 1960s, citizens agreed that Canada needed a national flag. However, there were many arguments about the design.

A flag committee voted on three flag designs. One design included the Union Jack. The second design was two vertical red bars on either side, with a single maple leaf on a white vertical bar in the centre. The third design was three maple leaves in a vertical bar between two vertical blue bars. After the first vote, the flag committee rejected the Union Jack flag. The committee voted again.

All members voted for the single maple leaf flag.

The single maple leaf flag was recommended as the design for the Canadian flag. However, the debate continued in Parliament, on television, and on the radio. In a democracy, the members of Parliament follow a rule called "Closure." Leon Balcer, a Québec Conservative, invited the Liberal government to use Closure. Every person's speaking time would be limited to 20 minutes. The parliamentary debate started

■ *The official credit for Canada's flag design is given to a parliamentary committee.*

on June 15, 1964, and lasted for 37 sitting days.

At 2:00 a.m. on December 15, 1964, Parliament accepted the flag committee's choice of a flag design. On January 28, 1965, Queen Elizabeth signed a royal proclamation making the single maple leaf Canada's flag. The flag was officially raised on February 15, 1965.

Mapping the Growth of Canada

The Confederation of Canada was created in 1867 with the union of Ontario, Québec, New Brunswick, and Nova Scotia. Since 1867, Canada has continued to grow. It now contains ten provinces and three territories.

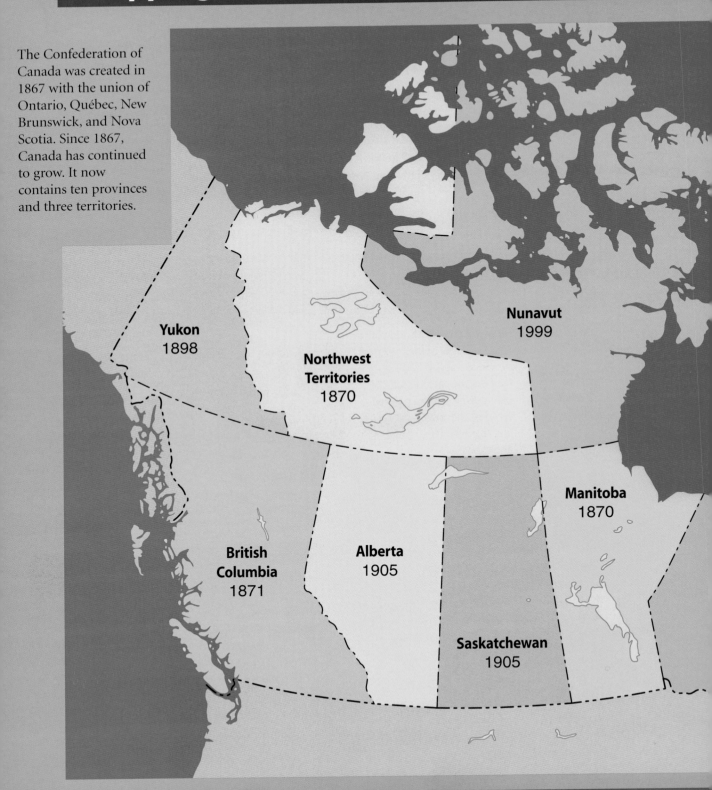

Yukon
1898

Northwest
Territories
1870

Nunavut
1999

British
Columbia
1871

Alberta
1905

Saskatchewan
1905

Manitoba
1870

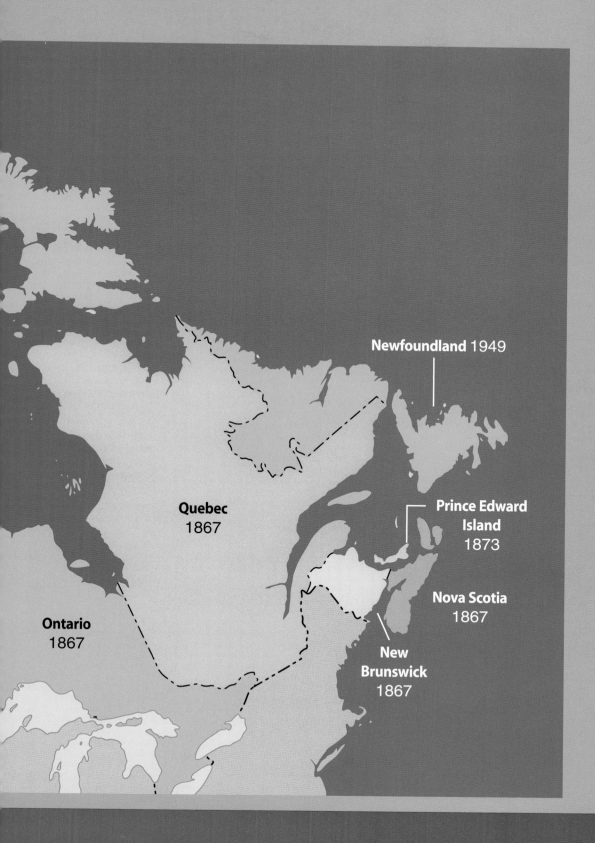

Newfoundland 1949

Quebec
1867

Prince Edward
Island
1873

Nova Scotia
1867

Ontario
1867

New
Brunswick
1867

Arctic Sovereignty

Canada's development from 1867 to the present has been a series of steps that have increased Canada's legal and practical sovereignty. However, no nation can be completely sovereign. All countries must interact with other nations over matters such as trade and transportation.

Sometimes the sovereignty of one nation to control its own affairs will be challenged by the sovereignty of another nation to act in its citizens' best interests.

The Canadian Arctic provided the setting for such a conflict of sovereign rights between Canada and the United States.

Early explorers came from Europe to Canada looking for a waterway that would allow them to bypass North America on their way to the Orient. For hundreds of years, explorers looked for a Northwest Passage, but they did not discover the passage until the nineteenth century. Eventually, it was discovered

> **Early explorers came to Canada looking for a waterway that would allow them to bypass the continent on their way to the Orient.**

> ■ *Canada claimed formal boundaries in the Arctic between 1970 and 1987. In 1880, Great Britain transferred its Arctic possessions to Canada—including undiscovered islands adjacent to this territory.*

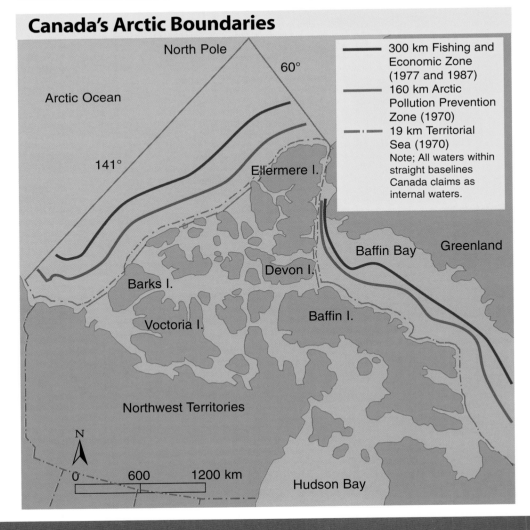

Canada's Arctic Boundaries

North Pole

60°

Arctic Ocean

141°

Ellermere I.

	300 km Fishing and Economic Zone (1977 and 1987)
	160 km Arctic Pollution Prevention Zone (1970)
	19 km Territorial Sea (1970)

Note; All waters within straight baselines Canada claims as internal waters.

Baffin Bay

Greenland

Devon I.

Barks I.

Baffin I.

Voctoria I.

Northwest Territories

N

0   600   1200 km

Hudson Bay

that the only way past North, Central, and Latin America was by sailing around them. One route was a long journey past the tip of South America. Another route was through Canada's Arctic waters. When the Panama Canal was built in Central America, a new and more useful route was created.

Since the Northwest Passage is rarely used, Canada placed little effort in defending its Arctic sovereignty. There are several problems involved with Arctic defence. The Canadian Arctic is a vast territory with a small population. In the Northwest Territories, the population density is about one person per 100 square kilometres. Since most people live in the capital, Yellowknife, there are very few people in outlying areas. The Arctic regions are almost uninhabited. This low population density makes it difficult for Canada to maintain an active and continuous presence, or even to know what is happening in isolated Arctic regions.

A second problem is that Canada does not have the military power to support its claims to certain parts of the Arctic. The Russian Federation, formerly the Soviet Union, also claims sovereignty over its Arctic territory. It protects its claim with ten icebreakers, including seven year-round nuclear-powered ships. Russians allow merchant shipping to use its Arctic waters, but they place their own pilots on board these ships to guide them through. Canada has twenty-one icebreakers strong enough to cope with the Arctic's severe winters. The Canadian Coast Guard operates nineteen of the twenty-one Canadian icebreakers.

Canada's north is patrolled by a 4,000-person unit known as the Canadian Rangers. This unit consists of Inuit hunters. They are expected to report any suspicious activities.

Canada persists in its claim to the Arctic territory. There are many reasons why the territory is valuable. If a war ever broke out between the United States and a country of the Commonwealth of Independent States, for example, the area would be the shortest route for a missile attack.

The region is also important as a potentially wealthy resource for offshore oil, gas, and mineral deposits. As well, it is one of the world's last untouched wilderness areas.

■ *The Canadian Arctic is sparsely populated. About 88,000 of Canada's 30 million residents live in the Arctic.*

Despite the Arctic's importance, Canada has found it difficult to exert a firm claim over the area. Canada's sovereignty comes into question because it cannot physically defend its claims. Canada lacks the naval strength, financial resources, and political will to defend the area against a strong power such as the United States, should it choose to challenge the Canadian claim.

The Northwest Passage

■ *The Canadian Arctic covers 26 million square kilometres. Only 8 million square kilometres are land. The rest is sea.*

In 1951, the International Court of Justice ruled that when coastlines are deeply indented with an **archipelago** of offshore islands, a nation could simply draw straight lines across the bays and between the tips of the islands to mark its boundaries. This system was further reinforced by the Law of the Sea Conference in 1982. This ruling allowed Canada to define its territorial boundaries in the North.

Canada used the so-called "straight baseline" ruling to draw a line around the Arctic islands. Canada then declared that all territory inside this line was Canadian. This defined territory included the Northwest Passage.

The United States does not recognize Canada's sovereignty over the passage.

The United States suggests that Canada is misreading the Law of the Sea and that Canada would lose a petition to the World Court to determine its boundary. The United States also believes Canada cannot limit access to the Northwest Passage because they see the passage as an international waterway.

The first test to Canada's sovereignty took place on August 24, 1969. The *Manhattan*, a Humble Oil Company tanker, and the *Staten Island*, a U.S. Coast Guard ship, set sail from the United States for the Northwest Passage. They were to determine if the passage was navigable for even part of the year.

When Canada was informed of the voyage, the federal government insisted that the Canadian Coast Guard

■ *In August 1994, the Canadian icebreaker, the* **Louis St. Laurent,** *escorted the American coast guard's* **Polar Sea** *to the North Pole.*

icebreaker *John A. Macdonald* accompany the *Manhattan*. Canada also placed an official representative and a Department of Transport observer on board the *Manhattan*. The *Manhattan* reached its destination at Prudhoe Bay, Alaska, in late September, making it the first commercial ship to negotiate the Northwest Passage.

As a result of the *Manhattan* voyage, the federal government passed the Territorial Seas Extension Act in 1970, which widened Canada's territorial seas from 4.8 to 19.3 kilometres from its coastlines. This act gave Canadians control over Atlantic and Pacific entrances to the Northwest Passage. The government also passed the Arctic Waters Pollution Act, which states that Canada's antipollution laws would apply to ships within 160 kilometres of its borders. The United States does not acknowledge Canadian law in this area. Although the United States accepts Canada's sovereignty over the Arctic islands, it defends its right to travel freely in international waterways.

Most U.S. concerns stem from fears about national security. For years, the American government feared that Soviet nuclear submarines patrolling beneath the Arctic ice might launch an attack on American cities. Another concern was economic. If Alaska's oil and gas fields were to be developed, transporting these resources by sea would be cheaper and quicker than taking other routes.

In 1985, Canada faced a second major challenge to its Arctic sovereignty. The United States sent its Coast Guard icebreaker the *Polar Sea* through the Northwest Passage without permission. The Canadian government informed the U.S. government that Canada objected to the action. After reviewing the U.S. need to patrol the area, the Canadian government granted its permission.

Opposition parties and Canadian nationalists were quick to protest this decision. Inuit and Council of Canada representatives even chartered an airplane and dropped a canister containing Canadian flags and messages onto the *Polar Sea*, requesting that the U.S. ship turn back.

In reaction to public outrage, Joe Clark, Minister of External Affairs, declared that while the voyage did not hurt the country's interests, it would not be repeated. He declared that Canada would pursue greater defence of its Arctic waters.

FURTHER UNDERSTANDING
Icebreakers

Icebreakers are heavy ships designed to break the thick ice in Arctic and Antarctic waters. Modern icebreakers are made of steel. They have a double hull and a rounded bow. The rounded bow enables an icebreaker to rise up on top of the ice. This allows the weight of the ship to break through ice much like a sledgehammer breaks through cement. Russian and U.S. icebreakers are able to break through 1.8- to 2.1-metres thick ice. Icebreakers are very expensive to build and operate. They are also uncomfortable to ride in—breaking through the ice causes constant vibration and noise. Still, these powerful boats have made it possible to sail through polar waters with greater ease and fewer tragedies.

Trudeau Foreign Policy Review

The Trudeau Review was important because it helped define Canada's foreign policy as independent from American and British domination.

In 1972, American President Richard Nixon and Prime Minister Pierre Trudeau signed an agreement to protect the Great Lakes from pollution.

By the 1960s, Canada had established its own niche in international affairs. Canadian foreign policy had developed a character of its own, although it was often securely tied to the foreign policy concerns of its allies.

Although Canada and the United States came into conflict occasionally, Canadian foreign policy had become very closely linked to its American neighbours. However, as American global involvements in places such as Vietnam, Cuba, and China became increasingly controversial, many Canadians questioned this closeness. Many believed that Canada was losing control of its own international position and becoming a satellite of the United States.

In 1968, Pierre Trudeau began his term as prime minister with an extensive review of Canadian foreign policy goals and directions.

The review, *Foreign Policy for Canadians*, appeared in 1970 with a statement governing the direction of Canada's international actions and commitments. Canadian foreign policy was to foster economic growth, safeguard sovereignty, work for peace and security, promote social justice, enhance the quality of life, and ensure a harmonious natural environment. Canada's foreign policy has followed the guidelines specified by this review in many ways since 1970.

Strengthened ties with Europe were sought to lessen Canadian dependence on the United States. Canada began to seek better economic and cultural relations with Pacific Rim countries such as Japan, especially in light of their growing populations. These populations offered enormous potential markets for Canadian products and services. The Trudeau Review stated that Canada should avoid military commitments in the Pacific Rim and provide more foreign aid. The policy suggested that Canada should build on the positive involvements begun through the Commonwealth and Colombo Plan to capitalize on the Pacific's position as a growing power.

The plan suggested that Canada should also seek more contact with Latin American countries such as Chile. Not only do they present an enormous market for Canadian exports, but they are a possible ally in the face of American influence in the southern hemisphere.

The Trudeau Review reaffirmed Canadian support of foreign aid programs. The report suggested that Canada should diversify its aid to other bodies than those served by the United Nations and the Commonwealth. Trudeau prophesied the importance of this last priority in a 1968 speech: "We must recognize that, in the long run, the overwhelming threat to Canada will come not from foreign investments or foreign ideologies, or even with foreign nuclear weapons. It will come instead from the two-thirds of the people of the world who are steadily falling further and further behind in their search for a decent standard of living."

IN-DEPTH

The Turbot War

As a way to extend its international influence and protect its own interests, Canada belongs to many international organizations. One of these is the Northwest Atlantic Fisheries Organization (NAFO), a regional organization that sets policies and mediates conflict with respect to fishing practices in the northwest Atlantic. In 1995, NAFO set quotas for the amount of turbot that Canadian boats and boats from other countries could catch. This was done to ensure the continuation of what is now a rapidly depleting fish stock. Turbot stocks are increasingly important to Canada. Since the collapse of the cod industry, they have been the mainstay of Atlantic fisheries.

Spain and Portugal challenged this quota through the European Union (EU), an organization that represents its member countries in trade matters. While the EU deliberated the quota question, Spanish and Portuguese boats continued to catch turbot beyond their quota. In March of 1995,

Canadian fisheries patrol boats fired warning shots across the bow of the Spanish trawler *Estai* and arrested the ship and its crew for overfishing. This sparked the "Turbot War." Following the seizure, the EU negotiated with Canada, and in exchange for a higher percentage of the

■ *Fisheries Minister Brian Tobin ordered patrol boats to harass and arrest Spanish trawlers.*

quota, the EU agreed to help enforce conservation rules in the disputed waters.

Yet there was evidence that Spanish trawlers continued to break the rules until the tentative agreement was formalized. Canadian fishing patrol boats also continued to board trawlers to check for illegal fishing equipment and the size of catches.

Patriation of the Constitution

Although Canada had been an active middle power and had conducted its affairs independently since World War I, it was still not completely sovereign. Prior to 1982, more than twenty amendments were made to the British North America Act. However, every time the Canadian government wanted to make an amendment, it needed the permission of the British Parliament. Canada was the only fully independent country that had to ask another country for permission to change its own Constitution.

In 1980, Trudeau announced his intention to **patriate** Canada's Constitution, "bringing home" the power to change and amend the Constitution without British involvement. Trudeau started negotiations with the provinces to reform the Constitution. The largest stumbling block was a clause left out of the British North America Act: an amending formula. The federal and provincial governments had to now agree upon how much power each government would have in any proposed amendments to the Constitution. During these negotiations, the federal government antagonized many provinces by its demands for more federal powers.

Many meetings were held between the federal and provincial governments to resolve their disagreements. The amending formula proved to be a difficult point to negotiate. The provinces could not agree on an amendment process. Some provinces wanted the right to veto, or disallow, any amendment they did not like.

In 1980, Prime Minister Trudeau announced that, if the provinces could not come to some agreement, the federal government would patriate Canada's Constitution on its own, without provincial consent.

Eight provinces were opposed to Trudeau's constitutional resolution:

Prime Minister Pierre Trudeau and Queen Elizabeth II signed Canada's Constitution on April 17, 1982.

PROFILE

Pierre Trudeau (1919–2000)

Pierre Trudeau became a celebrity before he was elected prime minister in 1968. During "Trudeaumania," as many as 16,000 people attended rallies for Trudeau.

Trudeau passed the Official Languages Act in 1969, making both French and English Canada's official languages. In 1970, the Front de Libération du Québec (FLQ) used violence to express their separatist ideals during the October Crisis. Trudeau invoked the War Measures Act.

Trudeau won the 1972 election with a minority government, but he won a majority government during another election in 1974. He battled inflation and tried to create jobs. In 1979, Trudeau lost the election to Conservative Joe Clark. Eight months later, Members of Parliament passed a vote of non-confidence in Clark's leadership, and another election was called. Trudeau agreed to return as Liberal leader and won the 1980 election.

Trudeau introduced the Constitution Act and the Charter of Rights and Freedoms in 1982. He resigned from office in 1984.

Pierre Trudeau served the third-longest term as prime minister of Canada.

Québec, Alberta, Manitoba, Prince Edward Island, Newfoundland, British Columbia, Saskatchewan, and Nova Scotia. Sometimes called the "Gang of Eight," they expressed their disapproval and appealed Trudeau's move in court. They also launched a public relations campaign in Canada and Great Britain against the federal government position.

Trudeau finally agreed to submit his resolution to Canada's Supreme Court. The Court decided that, although Trudeau was legally entitled to patriate the Constitution without provincial agreement, his actions went against Canada's constitutional conventions.

In November 1981, another round of bargaining began. Unfortunately, there was little agreement among the provinces. The deadlock was finally broken after several premiers held an informal meeting in a kitchen pantry as they took a break from formal meetings.

After many hours of hard bargaining, consensus for the new plan was achieved. There was one important exception. Premier of Québec René Lévesque refused to accept the agreement. He stated that the new Constitution threatened French Canada's cultural survival.

The Constitution Act of 1982 brought the Constitution under Canadian control. The agreement had three parts. It included the existing components of the British North America Act, introduced an amending formula, and included a Charter of Rights and Freedoms. Canada was finally established as a fully independent nation.

Amending Formulas

An amending formula is a set of rules used to make changes to a constitution. Canada partially settled the amending formula debate by including an amending formula in the Constitution Act 1982. Canada has several formal and informal amending procedures. There are eight formal procedures included in the Constitution for dealing with different types of constitutional amendments and a variety of informal procedures.

The first formal procedure is the general, or 7/50, amending procedure. This amending procedure relates to proportionate representation in the House of Commons, some matters related to the Senate and the Supreme Court of Canada, and new provinces. These types of amendments require the consent of the Senate and the House of Commons, and the consent of at least seven provincial legislatures that represent at least 50 percent of the Canadian population.

The second formal procedure is the opting out amending procedure. In this procedure, if an amendment affects the legislative powers, proprietary or other rights or privileges of the legislature or

As minister of justice, Jean Chrétien signed the Constitution Act 1982. This act included an amending formula, but it did not resolve debate about amendments.

government of a province, that province can opt out of the amendment.

The third formal procedure is a variation on the 7/50 procedure. In cases where an amendment will result in the transfer of "provincial legislative powers relating to education or other cultural matters from provincial legislatures to Parliament," one or more of the provinces may opt out. Any province opting out is eligible to receive "reasonable compensation" from the federal government.

The fourth formal procedure is the unanimity rule. This amending procedure relates to the Queen or her Canadian representatives, the composition of the Supreme Court of Canada, or changes to the amending formula itself. This type of amendment requires consent from both houses of Parliament and every provincial legislature.

The fifth formal procedure is used when the amendment affects one or more provinces but not all of them. This type of amendment requires consent from both houses of Parliament and the legislatures of the provinces affected by the amendment.

The sixth formal procedure is used when an amendment relates to the executive government of Canada—the Cabinet—or the Senate and House of Commons. These amendments only require the consent of Parliament.

The seventh formal procedure relates to amending provincial constitutions. In this procedure, amending the constitution of a province only requires the consent of the provincial legislature.

The eighth formal procedure requires federal and provincial governments to consult with representatives of the

Aboriginal Peoples of Canada before passing amendments that affect them.

Informal amending procedures are often used when the formal procedures are considered rigid and unworkable. Constitutional change can occur when the courts interpret existing constitutional provisions. For example, the Supreme Court of Canada ruled that all parties to Confederation would have to negotiate secession if a clear majority of the population of Québec voted in favour of a clear question on independence. Also, Parliament can pass legislation that alters constitutional rules. For example, the amending formula has been changed by legislation that requires a referendum before an amendment is addressed by a formal amending procedure.

■ *Provincial governments make decisions in legislative buildings located in their capital cities. Ontario's legislature is located in Queen's Park, Toronto.*

The Meech Lake Accord

Although Québec had not signed the Constitution Act and its Charter of Rights and Freedoms, constitutional negotiations were not over. The difference with the negotiations after 1982 was that now negotiations were entirely Canada's own—Great Britain was no longer involved.

Liberal Premier of Québec Robert Bourassa offered a set of conditions necessary to secure Québec's participation in the Constitution. On April 30, 1987, in a meeting at Meech Lake, the provincial premiers agreed to these conditions, resulting in the Meech Lake Accord.

The Accord recognized Québec as a distinct society and confirmed Canada's **bilingual** nature. It confirmed the provinces' right to opt out of shared-cost programs and to receive financial compensation for doing so. Meech Lake gave the provinces more control over immigration and agreed to appoint Supreme Court judges suggested by

the provinces. The Accord also proposed that any changes proposed to Canada's central institutions required unanimous agreement from all provinces.

The deadline by which the federal government and all ten provinces had to pass the Accord was June 23, 1990. As the deadline approached, Manitoba, Newfoundland, and New Brunswick had still not passed the Accord.

The province of Newfoundland would not pass the Accord without time to debate it in its legislature. Newfoundland wanted to conduct a referendum to obtain the opinions of its citizens about the details of the proposal.

The Manitoba Legislature also did not pass the Accord. In Manitoba, Member of the Legislature Elijah Harper held up the Manitoba Legislature on behalf of Canada's Aboriginal Peoples and refused to let the Accord pass. Constitutional amendments can only be passed by the Manitoba legislature after public consultation. The only way to override this rule is if the legislature

■ *Prime Minister Brian Mulroney proudly announced that the premiers had reached an agreement that resolved constitutional grievances on April 30, 1987. However, on June 23, 1990, Newfoundland and Manitoba refused to sign the Meech Lake Accord.*

Elijah Harper

Elijah Harper was the first treaty Indian ever elected to Manitoba's legislature. Born in northeastern Manitoba, he entered provincial politics in 1981 when he joined the legislature.

Harper opposed the Meech Lake Accord when it was created in 1987. The Accord did not provide for Aboriginal self-government, and it did not give Aboriginal Peoples the same recognition as English and French cultures. Harper objected to these omissions and believed the Accord would prevent Aboriginal Peoples from improving their way of life. As a result, Harper became the voice for Aboriginal Peoples and set out to stall the Accord's passage in the Manitoba Legislature. If the Accord was not passed by all ten provinces by June 23, 1990, a completely new agreement would have to be reached.

In June 1990, Premier Gary Filmon tried to bypass public hearings on the Accord. He wanted to speed up the Accord's passage, but he failed to give the legislature's members the required 2 days' notice before making the motion.

Although nearly everyone in the legislature ignored the lack of notice, Harper did not. He waited quietly in the legislature holding an eagle feather and a rule book. His feather represented peace and strength, and his rule book gave him an outlet by which to stop the process.

Harper said "no" to Filmon's motion in favour of the Accord six times. Thousands of Manitobans began notifying the government that they wanted to express their opinions about the Meech Lake Accord at public hearings. In the end, the Meech Lake Accord did not pass in Manitoba.

Harper's actions inspired Aboriginal Peoples, and they pressured politicians to place Aboriginal issues on the constitutional agenda. Aboriginal Peoples demanded greater recognition of treaty rights and more control over their schools, health care, and justice systems.

Harper was elected a Liberal member of Parliament for Manitoba in 1993.

Prime Minister Jean Chrétien appointed Harper Commissioner for the Indian Claims Commission in 1998.

votes unanimously in favour of a resolution. Harper's "no" vote, therefore, had the power to stop Manitoba's acceptance of the Accord, contributing to the Accord's failure.

Harper and other Aboriginal leaders were concerned that Aboriginal Peoples had not been given the same recognition French and English **cultures** received and that Aboriginal Peoples had not been included in the Accord's negotiations. The clause, which gave Québec status as a distinct society,

concerned many people as it seemed to privilege Québec above the other provinces. Some feared that Québec would have more power in Canada than any other province or territory.

The Accord failed to become law. Québec politicians stated that the province would not attend any future constitutional meetings unless they were granted the powers the provinces agreed upon at Meech Lake.

The Charlottetown Accord

■ *Joe Clark served as minister of constitutional affairs from 1991 to 1993.*

The next round of constitutional negotiations began soon after Meech Lake's failure. The leaders of four Aboriginal organizations, both territorial governments, and the premiers of all provinces except Québec entered the new set of discussions.

On July 7, 1992, Minister of Constitutional Affairs Joe Clark announced that his negotiating team had agreed on a package of constitutional proposals. The package was scheduled for approval at a first ministers meeting in Charlottetown, Prince Edward Island.

The Charlottetown Accord included Meech Lake's provisions, with several significant additions. One addition was a reform to the Senate, a reform pushed through by mainly western provinces who wanted to see their region better represented in Canada's institutions. The reforms proposed that the Senate be elected, and be composed of an equal number of Senators from each province.

A second important change was achieved through Aboriginal participation in the talks. The Charlottetown negotiations saw the high profile participation of many Aboriginal leaders. Media attention went to charismatic Ovide Mercredi and the "Mothers of Confederation," a group of three northern Aboriginal political leaders—Nellie Cournoyea, Rosemarie Kuptana, and Mary Simon. The

Aboriginal leaders received assurances of Aboriginal self-government, rectifying the problems that had caused Harper to reject the Meech Lake Accord.

However, the Charlottetown Accord was vague in several areas. For example, Aboriginal self-government was promised, but the details of how self-rule would unfold were missing. A section recognizing Québec as a distinct society was in place, without defining the practical implications of "distinctness." Some provinces feared the vagueness of the clause would later be interpreted to give Québec too much power.

Québec had more specific concerns with the proposal. The province objected to the Senate reform because it meant a reduction in Québec's seats in the Senate from twenty-four to eight.

On November 1, 1990, Prime Minister Brian Mulroney announced a round of cross-country public hearings called the Citizen's Forum on National Unity. This type of forum was unprecedented in Canadian history. The consultation prepared Canadians to make a decision about the Charlottetown Accord in 1992.

On October 26, 1992, Canadians were asked to vote for or against the Charlottetown Accord in a national referendum. Seventy-five percent of Canada's eligible voters cast a ballot. The Accord was rejected by six provinces—Prince Edward Island, Québec, Manitoba, Saskatchewan, Alberta, and British Columbia—and one territory—Yukon. An overall majority of Canadians rejected the Accord. Nationally, 54.2 percent of voters voted "no"; 44 percent voted "yes."

In the aftermath of the referendum, many people predicted that some of the Accord's clauses would be implemented anyway. Many, such as the proposed reforms to Aboriginal self-government, could be implemented without constitutional amendments.

DOCUMENT

The Canada Clause

The Canada Clause was a controversial section of the Charlottetown Accord.

The following are highlights from the Canada Clause:

2. (1) The Constitution Act, 1867, is amended by adding the following section:
   The Constitution of Canada, including the Canadian Charter of Rights and Freedoms, shall be interpreted in a manner consistent with the following fundamental characteristics:
   (a) Canada is a democracy committed to a parliamentary and federal system and to the rule of law;
   (b) The aboriginal peoples of Canada, being the first peoples to govern this land, have the right to promote their language, cultures and traditions; and to ensure the integrity of their societies; and their governments constitute one of three orders of government in Canada;
   (c) Québec constitutes within Canada a distinct society, which includes a French-speaking majority, a unique culture and a civil law tradition;
   (d) Canadians and their governments are committed to the vitality and development of official language minority communities throughout Canada;
   (e) Canadians are committed to racial and ethnic equality in a society that includes citizens from many lands who have contributed, and continue to contribute, to the building of a strong Canada that reflects its cultural and racial diversity;
   (f) Canadians are committed to a respect for individual and collective human rights and freedoms of all people;
   (g) Canadians are committed to the equality of female and male persons...;
   (h) Canadians confirm the principle of the equality of the provinces at the same time as recognizing their diverse characteristics;
2. (2) The role of the legislature and government of Québec to preserve and promote the distinct society of Québec is affirmed.

Time Line

1763 The Treaty of Paris gives Canada (New France and Acadia) to England.

1774 The Québec Act guarantees religious freedom for Roman Catholic colonists.

1784 United Empire Loyalists arrive in Canada.

Queen Victoria

1791 The Constitution Act grants representative government with limited powers for elected representatives. The act divides Québec into Upper and Lower Canada.

1818 The 49th parallel becomes the British North America/U.S. border.

1841 The Act of Union unites Upper and Lower Canada.

1848 Responsible government is established in Nova Scotia and Canada.

1857 Queen Victoria names Ottawa as Canada's capital.

1867 The confederation of Nova Scotia, New Brunswick, Québec, and Ontario forms the Dominion of Canada.

1867 Sir John A. Macdonald becomes Canada's first prime minister.

1869 Newfoundlanders decide not to join Confederation.

1870 The province of Manitoba is created.

1871 British Columbia joins Confederation.

1885 The transcontinental railway is completed.

1900 The federal immigration policy entices Eastern Europeans to the Canadian West.

1905 The provinces of Saskatchewan and Alberta are formed.

1914 Canada automatically enters World War I when Great Britain declares war on Germany.

1917 Income tax is introduced by the federal government as a "temporary wartime measure."

1918 Under the War Measures Act, the manufacture and sale of intoxicating beverages is prohibited in Canada.

1949 Newfoundland joins Confederation and becomes Canada's tenth province.

1960 The Quiet Revolution begins in Québec. The Canadian Bill of Rights is approved by Parliament.

1965 On January 28, 1965, Queen Elizabeth signs a royal proclamation making the single maple leaf Canada's official flag.

1967 Canada celebrates its centennial.

1968 English and French become the official languages of the federal government.

1970 The War Measures Act is used in response to the October Crisis.

1980 Québec votes against separation in a referendum. *O Canada* becomes Canada's national anthem.

1982 The Constitution is patriated, and the Charter of Rights and Freedoms is enacted.

1990 Manitoba refuses to ratify the Meech Lake Accord because it provides no special status for Aboriginal Peoples.

1992 The Charlottetown Accord is not ratified in a national referendum.

1999 Nunavut becomes Canada's third territory.

Quiz (answers on page 47)

Multiple Choice

Choose the best answer in the multiple choice questions that follow.

1 What is Canada's form of government called?

a) a republic
b) a constitutional monarchy
c) a dictatorship
d) a social club

2 The border between Canada and the United States is located along what parallel?

a) 60th parallel
b) 38th parallel
c) 40th parallel
d) 49th parallel

3 Who was Canada's first prime minister?

a) William Lyon Mackenzie King
b) Louis-Joseph Papineau
c) Sir John A. Macdonald
d) William Lyon Mackenzie

4 What did the British North America Act, 1867 give Canada?

a) internal self-rule
b) the status of a colony
c) membership in the Commonwealth
d) total independence from Great Britain

5 Which groups were not included in negotiations to establish a Confederation?

a) French Canadians
b) farmers
c) Aboriginal Peoples and women
d) property owners

6 When was the Naval Bill passed?

a) 1867
b) 1914
c) 1939
d) 1910

Mix and Match

Match the description in column A with the correct terms in column B. There are more terms than descriptions.

A	B
1. Passed in 1914 at the beginning of World War I	a) Billy Bishop
2. Greatest Canadian victory in World War I	b) Canadian Rangers
3. Rejected by the majority of Canadians in a national referendum	c) Canada's official flag
	d) Treaty of Washington
4. They patrol Canada's north	e) War Measures Act
5. Third-greatest air ace of World War I	f) Meech Lake Accord
6. Became official in 1965	g) the battle of Vimy Ridge
	h) Canadian Bill of Rights
	i) Charlottetown Accord

Time Line

Find the appropriate spot on the time line for each event listed below.

A Manitoba joins Confederation.

B Nova Scotia, New Brunswick, Ontario, and Québec form the Dominion of Canada

C The single maple leaf becomes official flag.

D Manitoba refuses to ratify the Meech Lake Accord.

E The Constitution Act divides Québec into Upper and Lower Canada.

F The provinces of Alberta and Saskatchewan are formed.

1791 1

1841 The Act of Union unites Upper and Lower Canada.

1857 Queen Victoria names Ottawa as Canada's capital.

1867 2

1869 Newfoundland rejects Confederation.

1870 3

1871 British Columbia joins Confederation.

1885 The transcontinental railway is completed.

1905 4

1914 Canada automatically enters World War I when Great Britain declares war on Germany.

1917 Income tax is introduced as a temporary wartime measure.

1949 Newfoundland joins Confederation.

1965 5

1968 English and French become the official languages of the federal government.

1970 The War Measures Act is used to respond to the October Crisis.

1982 The Constitution is patriated.

1990 6

1992 The Charlottetown Accord is not ratified.

1999 Nunavut becomes Canada's third territory.

Further Research

Suggested Reading

Axworthy, Lloyd. *Navigating a New World: Canada's Global Future*. Toronto: Knopf Canada, 2003.

Francis, Douglas, Richard Jones, and Donald B. Smith. *Origins: Canadian History to Confederation*. Toronto: Harcourt Canada, 2000.

Cook, S. A., R. McLean, and K. O'Rourke. *Framing Our Past: Canadian Women's History in the Twentieth Century*. Montréal: McGill-Queen's University Press, 2001.

Mallory, Enid L. *The Remarkable Years: Canadians Remember the 20th Century*. Markham, ON: Fitzhenry & Whiteside, 2001.

Internet Resources

Canada: A People's History Online
http://www.history.cbc.ca
The online companion to CBC's award-winning television series on the history of Canada, as told through the eyes of its people. This multimedia Web site features behind-the-scenes information, games, puzzles, and discussion boards. The site is also available in French.

The Canadian Encyclopedia Online
www.thecanadianencyclopedia.com
A reference for all things Canadian. In-depth history articles are accompanied by photographs, paintings, and maps. All articles can be read in both French and English.

Some Web sites stay current longer than others. To find other Web sites that deal with Canada and its place in the global village, enter terms such as "Canadian Constitution," "Northwest Passage," and "World War I" into a search engine.

Glossary

archipelago: a group of many islands in a large body of water

autonomy: self-government

bilingual: a policy of recognizing and encouraging two official languages—in Canada, French and English

colonies: areas that are not independent but are controlled by a foreign state

communism: a system in which goods are owned by everyone and are available to all in need

conscription: a policy where individuals are forced by law to enlist in the armed forces

Crown: the government under a constitutional monarchy

cultures: the learned and shared ways of life of groups of people at a given time which include such things as language, customs, and beliefs

diversity: a variety

dominion: a self-governing nation of the Commonwealth of Nations

federalism: a political system in which powers are divided between a central government and other regional governments

humanitarian: promoting human welfare and social reform

identity: a key characteristic which people use to define or describe themselves

immigrants: people who come into a country or region to live

monarch: a person who reigns over a kingdom or empire

patriate: bringing all decision-making authority to the people living in the area governed by the decisions

sovereignty: a condition where a country or group of people has the authority to make independent decisions concerning their own welfare

symbols: simple ways of representing things

Answers

Multiple Choice	Mix and Match	Time Line
1. b)	1. e)	1. e)
2. d)	2. g)	2. b)
3. c)	3. i)	3. a)
4. a)	4. b)	4. f)
5. c)	5. a)	5. c)
6. d)	6. c)	6. d)

Index